Wired and Wonderful
Women in the World of Smart Home Technology

Megan Diane Lewis

Table of Contents

1. Introduction 2
2. Opening the Doors to Smart Homes: An Introduction 3
   - 2.1. The Dawn of Smart Homes 3
   - 2.2. Unfolding the Dimensions of Smart Homes 4
   - 2.3. Women Spearheading the Smart Home Revolution 5
3. The Journey so Far: History of Women in Tech 6
   - 3.1. Pioneering Women in Computing 6
   - 3.2. The Mother of Software Engineering 7
   - 3.3. Breaking Entry Barriers in the Corporate World 7
   - 3.4. Gender Shift in Computing 7
   - 3.5. The Vision of Inclusion 8
   - 3.6. Women in the Evolution of Smart Home Technology 8
4. The Architects of Assistance: Women Behind Digital Assistants 10
   - 4.1. The Revolution of Voice assistants: From Typing to Speaking 10
   - 4.2. Women Who Lead: Pioneers in the Field 11
   - 4.3. Their Marks on the Tech Landscape: Innovations in Digital Assistants 11
   - 4.4. Challenges Along the Way: Adaptation, Acceptance, and Advancements 12
   - 4.5. Legacies in Code: Inspiring Future Generations 12
5. Securing Modern Homes: Championing Home Automation Security 14
   - 5.1. Industry Opener: Women's Role in Home Automation Security 14
   - 5.2. Brave women taking charge 14
   - 5.3. Inception of Ingenious Creations 15
   - 5.4. Navigating Through Complex Challenges: 15

- 5.5. The Road Ahead: 16
- 6. Creating Comfort and Convenience: The World of Home Automation 17
  - 6.1. Building Automation Into Our Everyday Existence 17
  - 6.2. Women Leaders Making Strides in Home Automation 18
  - 6.3. Innovations Redefining Home Automation 18
  - 6.4. Breaking Down Barriers 19
- 7. Emerging Leaders: Meet the Women Steering the Smart Home Revolution 21
  - 7.1. Breaking into the Smart Home Scene 21
  - 7.2. Transforming Home Automation 22
  - 7.3. Revolutionizing Home Security 22
  - 7.4. Impact on Sustainable Living 23
  - 7.5. Challenging the Status Quo 23
- 8. Shaping the Future: Next-Gen Innovations by Women in Smart Home Tech 24
  - 8.1. The Advent of IoT and AI 24
  - 8.2. The Evolution of Voice Assistants 25
  - 8.3. Insights into Home Security Innovation 25
  - 8.4. Toward More Energy-Efficient Homes 26
  - 8.5. The Future is Inclusive 26
- 9. Breaking Barriers: Challenges Faced and Overcome 28
  - 9.1. Who Gets the Seat at the Table? 28
  - 9.2. The Gender Pay Gap: An Unfinished Business 29
  - 9.3. The Invisible Walls: Stereotypes and Perceptions 29
  - 9.4. Balancing Act: Career and Personal Demands 29
  - 9.5. From Discouragement to Encouragement: Transforming Education 30
- 10. Finding Balance: Personal Stories from Women in the Tech Industry 31

- 10.1. Triumphs and Trials: The Never-ending Learning Curve ... 31
- 10.2. Personal Lives in Perpetual Motion: Striking the Work-Life Balance ... 32
- 10.3. Wellness, a Silent Casualty: Revisiting Health and Happiness ... 32
- 10.4. The Power of Networks: Building Support Systems ... 33
- 10.5. The Never-Ending Balancing Act: Navigating the Way Forward ... 33

11. The Future is Bright: How Women are Reshaping the Technology Roadmap ... 34
    - 11.1. Protagonists of Progress: Women Pioneers in Technology ... 34
    - 11.2. Intelligent Abodes: Women Leading Home Innovation ... 35
    - 11.3. Advancing Past the Obstacles: Women Rising Against the Odds ... 36
    - 11.4. Shaping Tomorrow: The Path Ahead ... 36

We do not need magic to transform our world. We carry all the power we need inside ourselves already. We have the power to imagine better.

— J.K. Rowling

Chapter 1. Introduction

Dive into our special report, "Wired and Wonderful: Women in the World of Smart Home Technology." In an industry that's often perceived as male-dominated, you'll discover groundbreaking women rocking the helm, designing ingenious tools for an increasingly tech-driven domestic space. From creating intuitive voice assistants to building state-of-the-art security systems, these tenacious innovators are not just reshaping our homes, but also challenging the status quo. Exploring beyond the complex jargon and the maze of circuit-boards, we delve into the inspiring journeys of these trailblazers. Offering a conservative, yet engaging viewpoint into a tech-empowered world, this special report is a must-read for anyone interested in smart homes and the unsung female heroes behind them. Your outlook towards technology in home space will never be the same after experiencing this enlightening exploration.

Chapter 2. Opening the Doors to Smart Homes: An Introduction

The rapid evolution in the digital terrain has recently stumbled upon an intersection where the traditional concept of homes cross paths with advanced technology. This junction heralds the era of smart homes, an amalgamation that represents a seismic shift in how we dwell, live, and interact with our spaces. It orchestrates a symphony where cutting-edge technology dance in perfect harmony with your once mundane household chores, transposing them into intuitive and seamless processes.

2.1. The Dawn of Smart Homes

Smart homes owe their birthright to the futuristic vision that resonated amid the world fairs and science fiction of the mid-20th century. The Jetsons, a classic animated sitcom, presented the ultimate technologically advanced home that stole the show in the 1960s with its autonomous robots, holograms, and elaborate push-button or voice-activated devices. While for many, this was a footprint of imaginatively whimsical fiction, a select few viewed it as a beacon showing the way forward—the early stage blueprints of smart homes.

However, the actual realization of smart home technology stepped into our real-life canvas around the late 1990s, with the innovative endeavors of various tech companies. X10, a protocol for communication among electronic devices, pioneered the earliest phases of home automation. It applied existing power lines within the home to transmit digital data. Despite the limitations of X10 in terms of signal reliability and security concerns, it jolted the static notion of dwelling spaces, catapulting them toward a dynamic transformation.

2.2. Unfolding the Dimensions of Smart Homes

Smart homes can be seen as a multi-faceted reality which, akin to a prism, takes one element — in this case, the home — and reflects it back in a multitude of radiant, technicolor aspects.

Integrated Technology: One of the most revolutionary aspects of smart homes is the concept of Integrated Technology. Integrated Technology is a seamless blend of various emerging technologies such as IoT (Internet of Things), AI (Artificial Intelligence), and Machine Learning. It implements automatous technology in synchrony to bolster efficiency, productivity, energy conservation, and convenience in domestic space.

Interconnected Ecosystem: In a smart home, all the devices are part of an interconnected ecosystem. This ecosystem allows the devices to communicate and co-operate with each other in real-time, making it feasible for your coffee machine to prepare a cup for you when your alarm clock signals that you're awake.

Control: A smart home hands over unprecedented control to the homeowner. Using apps on their smartphone, one can control all connected devices remotely. Whether you wish to adjust the room temperature or monitor your home security while away, smart home technology bestows you with the power to do so with a simple tap.

Efficiency: Smart homes help conserve resources and cut costs by optimizing energy use. For instance, smart bulb technology allows the lighting system to adjust according to the natural light availability and occupancy in the room.

2.3. Women Spearheading the Smart Home Revolution

In a realm that originally resonated with the echoes of male-domination, women have emerged as inventors, leaders, and innovators. Their profound influence has inadvertently jabbed away any isomorphic preconceived notions about women's role in the tech industry. They have designed and implemented advanced tools in designated domestic spaces that amalgamate both functionality and finesse.

As we navigate further into this intriguing journey, we uncover the numerous inspiring women who have not only spurred the growth of smart home technology but also shattered the glass ceiling in the process. Let's plunge into this mesmerizing odyssey of innovation, transformation, and the sheer display of tenacity that has begun to redefine our perception of home and hearth.

Chapter 3. The Journey so Far: History of Women in Tech

The narrative of women in technology is one intricately intertwined with the very foundations of the evolution that the tech space has undergone over history. Not merely accessories to the sweeping tale of arms races in silicon and software, women have been principal actors, raising curtains, catalyzing revolutions, and charting the course of technological progress from behind the scenes and front.

3.1. Pioneering Women in Computing

As we trace our steps back in time, the critical role of women in technology makes itself visible. Women have been prodigious contributors to the field of computing, long before the term 'computer' was associated with an electronic device.

During World War II, a group of six women programmed the first all-electronic programmable computer, the ENIAC. Jean Jennings Bartik, Betty Snyder Holberton, Kathleen McNulty Mauchly Antonelli, Marlyn Wescoff Meltzer, Frances Bilas Spence, and Ruth Lichterman Teitelbaum were selected from a larger pool for their mathematical prowess. In a time when gender roles were highly stratified, these women punched holes into cards and rewired panels, manoeuvring around the manually set operations in an era pre-dating programming languages or tools.

3.2. The Mother of Software Engineering

Fast forward to the early 1960s, and we encounter a monumental figure in the history of women in tech: Margaret Hamilton. Her contributions to software engineering remain indelible and her role in the 1969 Apollo moon landing, immortal. Hamilton championed the concept of asynchronous software, priority scheduling and human-in-the-loop decision capability, which were all instrumental to the success of Apollo missions. She injected resilience and robustness into the software design, a trait that would later change the course of the Apollo 11 mission.

3.3. Breaking Entry Barriers in the Corporate World

While women were scripting the success stories of many pivotal tech moments, there were others who were breaking entry barriers in the corporate world. Ursula Burns rose up the ranks in the 1980s and 1990s, eventually becoming the first African-American woman CEO of a Fortune 500 company, Xerox, in 2009. She shattered glass ceilings and paved the path for many to follow, demonstrating that leadership in technology was not solely the domain of men.

3.4. Gender Shift in Computing

Sadly, a gender shift happened in the computing industry around the 1980s. An industry that owed so much to its pioneering women began to be gradually dominated by men, courtesy of personal computers being marketed more towards boys and men. This resulted in a disproportionately lower representation of women in the tech realm—a challenge that the industry grapples with even today.

3.5. The Vision of Inclusion

The new millennium set the stage where more women began to rise in the echelons of power, leading tech giants like HP, IBM, and Yahoo!. It was during this time that Sheryl Sandberg, COO of Facebook, famously brought to the forefront the issues of representation and gender equality in the tech-sphere with her book "Lean In". Her observations initiated an industry-wide conversation, and ever since, technology firms have been placing stronger emphasis on diversity, inclusion, and equal representation.

3.6. Women in the Evolution of Smart Home Technology

As we delve into the 21st century, a remarkable trend of women advancing home technology surfaces. Female tech innovators have been integral in developing smart home technologies, shaping and defining how we interact with our domestic spaces today. Be it intuitive voice assistants, intelligent climate control, smart security systems, automated cooking appliances, or connected lighting solutions, women innovators have pushed boundaries and driven the development of these technologies.

As we continue to move forward, it is clear that the journey of women in the realm of tech is far from complete. The baton has been passed on, and more young female innovators are reaching out eagerly to accept it, shaping the present and the future of smart homes and beyond.

This historical overview of women in technology stands as a testament that their contributions have been profoundly impactful over the eras, even amidst challenges. It is a vibrant tapestry of innovation, determination, breakthroughs, and leadership. It is also a continual reminder that the pursuit of gender equality in technology is not only a matter of social justice, but also a prerequisite for true technological innovation. Female participation and leadership in technology bring about holistic, diverse perspectives and approaches that represent and serve all of society's needs, fostering richer, more creative and inclusive solutions for the world's evolving technological landscape.

Undeniably, the journey so far has been fraught with both challenges and triumphs. What remains constant is the indomitable spirit of the women who have shaped—and continue to shape—the tech realm, pushing frontiers and driving the course of digital evolution.

Chapter 4. The Architects of Assistance: Women Behind Digital Assistants

Born in a world where technological sophistication is rapidly becoming the norm, digital voice assistants have become an integral part of our everyday lives. These voice-command devices have certainly revolutionized user-machine interaction, transforming archaic modes of input to a more organic form of communication: human speech. Spearheading this cutting-edge domain, a group of remarkable women have been etching their name in the annals of tech history with ground-breaking work in the realm of digital assistants. We keep our focus on such women who have been instrumental in pushing the boundaries, leveraging technological ascendance to their advantage, and scripting astounding success stories.

4.1. The Revolution of Voice assistants: From Typing to Speaking

The genesis of voice assistants can be traced back to the early nineties, with speech recognition technology slowly gaining popularity. However, it wasn't until the 21st century that the world witnessed a significant upswing in its usage and subsequent development. From helping visually impaired individuals to providing hands-free convenience to the masses, the voice assistants, also known as virtual assistants or AI assistants, have come a long way. Women have been at the epicenter of some of this seismic shift from typed to verbal inputs, making the process infinitely more interactive and captivating for end users.

4.2. Women Who Lead: Pioneers in the Field

There's no shortage of women who have punched a hole in the proverbial glass ceiling within this technological revolution. For example, Joelle Pineau, a leading AI researcher at Facebook, has played a pivotal role in creating software models for voice assistants that empower them with better human-like conversation capabilities. Her efforts in harnessing the power of reinforcement learning have signaled a new era of understanding between humans and machines.

Similarly, Jan Chong, a Lead Engineer at Apple, was instrumental in developing Siri. Chong's work on natural language processing and machine learning has contributed significantly to the evolution of Siri, making it a household name today.

In addition to these women, there are countless others like Aarthi Ramamurthy, Microsoft's Azure AI partner engineering manager who contributes to the development of Cortana.

4.3. Their Marks on the Tech Landscape: Innovations in Digital Assistants

The innovative contributions from these deft women have reshaped the landscape of digital assistance. The advent of voice recognition mixed with cutting-edge AI has enabled software products to imitate human interaction more authentically. This has profound implications for accessibility, convenience, and efficiency in everyday life, from setting alarms and managing our calendars to controlling an increasingly diverse array of smart home devices.

A prime exemplar of these sweeping changes is the

intercommunication between smart home devices, facilitated by voice technology. It's no longer a fantastical premise, having IoT devices communicate with us, and with each other, in everyday conversational language.

4.4. Challenges Along the Way: Adaptation, Acceptance, and Advancements

Despite these groundbreaking accomplishments, the path has not always been smooth. Technological adaptation and acceptance were among the primary challenges endured in the dawn of digital assistants. Much of society was initially hesitant to embrace this new mode of interaction, skeptical about privacy and accuracy.

However, through relentless dedication to advancement and a commitment to consumer education, these pioneering women have helped dismantle many of the initial hurdles faced by voice technology. Their efforts have fostered improved understanding, openness, and acceptance of these devices, setting the stage for continued exploration and innovation in the field.

4.5. Legacies in Code: Inspiring Future Generations

The enduring legacy of these pioneering women transcends the realms of programming languages and circuit boards. They have also paved the way for future generations of female tech enthusiasts. They embody a powerful message of resilience and dynamism, proving that success in the realm of technology is not bounded by gender.

Their stories, laden with passion, determination, and intellect, cement their positions as role models for young girls who aspire to make it big in tech. Their success has done more than just blaze a new technological trail – it has inspired a whole generation of women to follow the same path, thus fostering greater diversity and innovation in the tech industry.

In conclusion, women have not only mirrored the voting rights motto of 'Voice and Vote", but have adapted it to the quintessential 21st-century axiom of 'Voice and Command'. As we traverse forward in the world of tech, let's celebrate the remarkable women who have taken the helm in the world of voice assistants, transforming our lives and our homes. Their tireless pursuit of innovative solutions and their drive to create accessible and interactive tech make them not only architects of assistance but architects of the future.

Chapter 5. Securing Modern Homes: Championing Home Automation Security

Today, as home automation systems burgeon, witnessing an unprecedented growth and acceptance rate, it is incumbent on us to take a deep and extensive gaze into the realm of home automation security. Spearheading this vital and a tad convoluted area, brave and innovative women are redesigning paradigms of safety in the modern smart homes.

5.1. Industry Opener: Women's Role in Home Automation Security

As we delve into the intricacies, it's essential to shed light on women's instrumental role at the vanguard of smart home security systems. Beyond the tedious wiring, complex programming, and state-of-the-art technological tools, lies the genius of these creative minds. From product design to implementation and maintenance, they are championing every stratum of this smart ecosystem, challenging archaic notions, and promising an improved and secure living environment.

5.2. Brave women taking charge

Among these pioneers in the smart home security space, a few names standout. One such is Anne Ferguson, the Vice-President of Marketing at Alert 360. Ferguson's prime focus revolves around personalized home automation systems that integrate seamless security solutions. Catering to various user specific needs, her innovative approach underscores the importance of inclusivity in tech-driven security systems.

In another corner of the world, you'll find Jodi Schiller, creating ripples in the automation industry. As the Founder of HomeKit Heroes, she is revolutionizing home security, stirring a blend of emerging technologies like the Internet of Things (IoT), centered around Apple's HomeKit framework.

5.3. Inception of Ingenious Creations

It is crucial here to grasp the intuitive and user-friendly security products emerging under these women's aegis. Think of smart locks developed under Ferguson's leadership, enabling remote access and real-time monitoring through simple and intuitive applications. It stands as a testament to women's potential in shaping futuristic tech designs.

Schiller, on the other hand, is directing her efforts towards integrating AI into home security systems. With the use of AI-driven facial recognition, she aims to make trespassing detection more accurate and efficient. Her products, a melange of convenience and security, are breaking new frontiers in home automation.

5.4. Navigating Through Complex Challenges:

Creating robust and reliable home automation security systems is no easy feat. These women face numerous challenges, including the tightrope walk between maintaining user privacy and ensuring maximum security. Balancing this delicate equilibrium reflects their ingenuity and resilience.

Moreover, they also endure challenges related to the scarcity of women in this predominantly male-dominated space. Battling stigmas and combating biases, these indefatigable women are redefining the leadership narrative in the tech landscape.

5.5. The Road Ahead:

Looking ahead, the future glows bright as women continue to leave indelible imprints on the smart home security industry. Their innovative approach, coupled with a user-centric vision, is helping build an exciting era of technology-led home security. Through their tenacious spirit and techno-creative prowess, they are not only disrupting conventional security standards but also seeding the desire for safe innovation within the technology realm.

In conclusion, as home automation becomes an inherent part of our lives, it is these revolutionary women, championing the home automation security, that provide the much-needed assurance of safety. For every tangle of wires, every complex system, every innovation in this tech-infused reality, there is a tenacious woman navigating the maze, devising a strategy, solving a problem, and thus, ensuring that our smart-homes are not just comfort-filled but also secure. It is their tireless pursuit of a secure smart living that's painting a new tomorrow and offering a tribute to women's robust presence in the tech industry. This emergence of women trailblazers underpins their ever-increasing influence on the behavioral pattern of technology and its futuristic roadmap, the effects of which are profound and far-reaching.

Chapter 6. Creating Comfort and Convenience: The World of Home Automation

In the arena of home automation, convenience and comfort are intertwined, coalescing into a seamless synergy that bolsters the quality of our daily lives. This union is manifested in devices and systems so neatly incorporated into our surroundings that they almost become invisible, operating in the background to make our lives smoother and more streamlined. Nestled within this intricate ecosystem, a formidable cadre of women are leading the way, employing technology to craft experiences that bridge the gap between the human desire for ease and the unyielding march of technological progress.

6.1. Building Automation Into Our Everyday Existence

Underpinning most automation technology is the principle of simplifying and enhancing our interactions with the physical world. Here, smart home devices take center stage as subtle enablers of a seamless existence, busily whirring in the background of our lives, anticipating our needs, and responding flawlessly to meet them. These systems could range from smart lights that adjust the ambient settings based on time or weather, to voice-controlled thermostats that maintain optimal temperature without any human intervention.

Why are these tools increasingly popular? The answer lies in their innate ability to straddle the realms of efficiency and convenience. The pioneering women in this field often attribute much of their inspiration to the endless human pursuit of a frictionless life. Though the realm of automation was often seen to be an exclusive, inaccessible playground of mechanical wizards and coding gurus, these women are debunking that image, displaying that the power to create is not only wielded by a select few but is richly democratic and inclusive.

6.2. Women Leaders Making Strides in Home Automation

Delving into the arena of pioneers, we encounter a constellation of women striving to bring automation into every home and hearth. One striking professional in this realm is Alexa von Tobel, the founder of LearnVest, a tech platform designed to democratize financial planning and forethought. Von Tobel's trailblazing journey in the realm of fintech has led her to venture further into home automation with Cleo Capital, with a focus on using tech to streamline domestic chores and workload.

Another name to be reckoned with is Felicite Moorman. As the CEO of STRATIS IoT, she propels the charge in creating SaaS platforms for smart apartments and intelligent buildings, thus filling a niche traditionally overlooked in the smart home market. Moorman's overarching goal of intertwining technology with real estate has been revolutionary, grounding the vision of smart living in tangible, daily experiences.

6.3. Innovations Redefining Home Automation

Creating comfort and convenience, however, goes beyond merely inventing efficient tools. It's about nurturing a fine balance between human needs and the opportunities provided by technology. The challenge lies in distilling abstract human desires and comfort into tangible, responsive technology.

An example of this human-centered design approach is The Nadi Smart fitness pants developed by Billie Whitehouse and the innovative team at Wearable X. Guided by embedded technology, the yoga pants deliver haptic feedback to ensure accurate poses, almost like having a yoga instructor in the comfort of your home. The focus here is on fostering a personal and interactive experience that enhances user satisfaction and convenience.

Another striking example of this pursuit of a tailor-made automated experience is Tony Fadell's Nest Learning Thermostat. The unassuming device is a manifestation of the intertwined influence of automation and intuitive design. It learns the home owner's routines over time, maintaining the perfect temperature in an unobtrusive manner while saving fuel costs - an amalgam of comfort, convenience, and sustainability.

6.4. Breaking Down Barriers

These many successes, however, do not come easy. The journey of women in this tech-dominated field has been rife with challenges - often unseen and unaccounted for. From gaining mastery over the intricate labyrinths of technology to pitching their product ideas to often skeptical investors, these women have grappled with societal expectations and weathered criticism. At worst, their abilities and credentials are questioned, but what powers their journey is the sheer tenacity and the staunch belief in the transformative power of home automation to make everyday-life more conducive.

To conclude, home automation is not just about embedding machines into our lives, but about understanding an intricate matrix of people, their needs, their homes, and their contextual realities. The domain of home automation, thus, needs creators that combine empathy with innovation. This chapter about creating comfort and convenience offered insight into that journey, providing a nuanced perspective on the world of home automation led by a legion of powerful, creative women. The future of our homes spurred by their endeavor will be smarter, not just more connected, thus nurturing an environment that seamlessly blends comfort and convenience.

Chapter 7. Emerging Leaders: Meet the Women Steering the Smart Home Revolution

Emerging leaders in the world of smart home technology are not only reshaping the landscapes of their respective fields, but also altering the very perception of women in technology. This chapter presents a series of interviews and profiles highlighting women who are driving change and innovation within this industry.

7.1. Breaking into the Smart Home Scene

In an era defined by digital technology and innovation, several women stand out with significant contributions that have pioneered the evolution of smart homes. Their groundbreaking work has not only shifted the dynamic of traditionally male-dominated fields but has molded the world to sit up and recognize the influence and power of women in tech.

Dr. Patricia Scanlon is one such noteworthy name. Founder of SoapBox Labs, she has revolutionized the world of voice recognition technology. With an ever-increasing demand for voice-enabled smart home systems, Dr. Scanlon's company utilizes AI with impressive accuracy, enabling smooth integration into any smart home interface. Her technology has made it far easier to operate smart home devices, paving the way for a new era where voice commands a unique interactive approach.

Another inspiring figure is Anne Ferguson, the vice president of marketing at Alarm.com. Her work has played a pivotal role in developing and implementing IoT-based home security solutions.

Ferguson's innovative strategies have led to a surge in the adoption of smart home technology, demonstrating its practical benefits to the everyday homeowner.

7.2. Transforming Home Automation

The world of home automation is becoming increasingly user-friendly, thanks largely to the pioneering work of women like Yoky Matsuoka. As the VP of Google Nest, she is responsible for creating effective machine-learning programs to power today's smart homes. Matsuoka's vision involves building smart homes that not only respond to commands but learn from behaviour patterns to adapt to the needs of homeowners over time.

Caterina Fake, a co-founder of Flickr, and later, Findery, has made substantial contributions in terms of implementing location-based storytelling in smart devices. Fake's innovative approach to augmenting information to specific locations and objects provides an added dimension to how we interact with smart tech.

7.3. Revolutionizing Home Security

Home security has been an essential focal point in the development of smart homes, with the objective being not only to protect but to anticipate threats intelligently. Jamie Siminoff, the founder of Ring Inc., captures this perfectly. Her Wi-Fi-enabled video doorbells and cameras have brought about a radical change in how we view home security. By linking these devices to our smartphones, Siminoff's expansive vision offers control over security like never before.

7.4. Impact on Sustainable Living

The fusion of smart tech and sustainability is yet another area where women are leading the charge. Genevieve Beecham, the co-founder of G2 Microgrids, exemplifies this through the development of off-grid energy solutions for homes. By integrating Solar PV, wind turbines, and battery storage, Beecham's application of IoT in sustainable home energy offers a green alternative for tech-driven homes.

7.5. Challenging the Status Quo

Such strides in smart home technology have been revolutionary, but they are neither the end goal nor the ceiling. Women in tech continue to blaze trails, face challenges head-on, and take on roles that demand leadership, invention, and candid diversity. Jess Lee's incredible work as the CEO of Polyvore and later, Sequoia Capital, proves that women in technology are more than able to rise to the challenge, even in the face of traditional stereotypes and hurdles.

Each one of these accounts underlines the importance of recognizing the women steering the smart home revolution. Such recognition shines a light on the potential of women in the field, encouraging participation and providing inspirational role models for the next generation of women in technology. By spotlighting their achievements, we hope to encourage more women to take the step into this world, break the glass ceiling, and own the future. The smart home revolution is lucky to have these leaders, and we await its further evolution under their savvy guidance.

Chapter 8. Shaping the Future: Next-Gen Innovations by Women in Smart Home Tech

The future of smart home technology, powered by a wave of innovative women, promises to transform our lives in ways we're only beginning to imagine. Rid of traditional gender roles, these pioneering women are busting past barriers to create state-of-the-art appliances that simplify domestic duties, invest in the creation of more secure houses, and foster a more interactive and empowered living environment. This section of our extensive report aims to paint a vivid picture of how their pioneering work in smart home technology is shaping our shared tomorrows.

8.1. The Advent of IoT and AI

To understand just how revolutionary these innovations truly are, it's essential to unwrap the underlining developments in the foundation of smart home technology. The Internet of Things (IoT) and Artificial Intelligence (AI) form the core of these advances. IoT facilitates the connectedness of devices within the home, enabling quick and convenient command executions, while AI equips these devices with the aptitude to learn and adapt to user behaviors and preferences over time.

At the center of this IoT and AI revolution, we find women leading the charge. Jessica Tan, co-founder and CEO of a leading tech platform, for instance, propels broad adoption of IoT technologies among homes to make them 'smarter'. Further oven, Dr. Fei-Fei Li, a known computer scientist, elaborately works towards imbuing these interconnected devices with advanced AI capabilities to enhance their intuitive functionality and responsiveness. Dr. Li's work in particular has revolutionized the manner in which humans interact with their devices, enabling a seamless two-way communication channel.

8.2. The Evolution of Voice Assistants

No discussion about smart homes can forgo the significance of voice assistants. In a relatively short span of time, these digital companions have transformed from novelty items to indispensable components of our homes. Responding to both routine and spontaneous commands, they play an essential role in fostering an easy, interactive, and efficient living environment.

Women have been instrumental in crafting these virtual assistants to become more intuitive and responsive. Amazon's Echo was primarily designed by a team that heavily included women, under the leadership of Miriam Daniel, Vice President of Echo and Alexa devices at Amazon. Her vision was not just to create a voice-enabled device, but to install an integral member of the house that could ease the burden of mundane household tasks.

8.3. Insights into Home Security Innovation

The ease of life offered by smart homes doesn't end with convenience. Females innovators have also been at the helm of designing smart home security systems that offer peace of mind to residents by safeguarding their homes efficiently and effectively. Laura Dangerfield, Director of UX at AlertMedia, for instance, is working tirelessly to engineer control systems that not only detect potential threats in real-time but also device proactive safety measures.

8.4. Toward More Energy-Efficient Homes

With global warming increasingly posing a significant risk, the planet needs homes to become not only smarter but also greener. The world of smart home technology finds itself indebted to a multitude of women leading the way forward. Annie Eaton, CEO of Futurus, has been championing the cause for energy-efficient homes by incorporating IoT technologies that manage home heating, air conditioning, and electrical consumption in an eco-conscious manner.

8.5. The Future is Inclusive

The promise of future smart home technology lies not just in its capacity to learn, evolve, and respond to each command but to deliver an inclusive experience. To that effect, women are ensuring that everyone – irrespective of age, ability, or understanding of the technology – can enjoy the blessings of a smart home. GeriJoy's founder, Victor Wang, with his woman-led team, has built an elder-friendly tech platform, pushing the envelope on inclusivity in the smart home sector.

Creating a well-orchestrated symphony of diverse technological advancements, these pioneering women are directing us towards the next exciting era in the landscape of smart home technology. This in-depth examination of their work should drive us to not only appreciate their efforts but to ponder upon the future of the smart home world and how we'll interact with it. Allow yourself to imagine a world where your home isn't just a physical dwelling, but an intuitive entity that grows with and looks after you. This upcoming reality is thanks to the tenacity, vision, and ingenuity of women progressing the technological frontier.

Chapter 9. Breaking Barriers: Challenges Faced and Overcome

With a nod to the undeniable reality, it's crucial to recognize that the trailblazing journey of women in the smart home technology industry is strewn with challenges. Notwithstanding the transformative strides they're making, a closer appraisal reveals an array of barriers that these stalwart figures have needed to confront, and continue to do so, in this male-dominated sector.

9.1. Who Gets the Seat at the Table?

Let's start by shedding light on a fundamental hurdle, capturing the essence of gender inequality in the tech industry - representation and inclusivity. The proverbial 'seat at the table' in technology-driven boardrooms comes with difficulty for many women. Corporate norms, entrenched prejudices, and a deeply rooted 'boys club' mentality often act as detractors, causing women to climb an uphill battle for equal representation. An exhaustive analysis of Fortune 500 companies shows the telling figure, women hold less than a quarter of the leadership positions in prominent tech firms, a telling testament to a systemic issue.

Despite societal progress and enactment of gender equality laws, the reality remains disapposite. Overcoming the challenge of underrepresentation necessitates a culture shift, a tearing down of the walls of patriarchy, and an earnest commitment from companies to maintain gender diversity in their echelons.

9.2. The Gender Pay Gap: An Unfinished Business

Amidst the array of hurdles, the gender pay gap is a poignant sore and a clear-cut indication of the prevailing gender bias. Many accomplished women in smart home technology navigate through their careers, inventing, innovating, and leading, while being compensated less than their male counterparts for the same quantity and quality of work. Census data and reports underline that on average women earn merely 80 cents for every dollar earned by a man. This figure is a gross injustice and an ongoing challenge that needs concerted efforts to be tackled.

9.3. The Invisible Walls: Stereotypes and Perceptions

Stereotypically, the image of a techie is associated with a male figure - coding away in a basement, surrounded by circuits and tools. This widespread narrative continues to build invisible walls around women, subscribing them to certain roles, discouraging them from exploring and pursuing careers in tech-related fields. Overcoming this stereotyped perception is an enduring challenge and requires a relentless commitment to raise awareness and initiate deeper societal shifts in perspective.

9.4. Balancing Act: Career and Personal Demands

In an industry that demands persistent upgrades and perpetual learning due to its rapidly evolving nature, juggling career advancements with personal life commitments is yet another major challenge faced by women. Striking a balance between family responsibilities and maintaining an edge in rapidly shifting technological paradigms prove a taxing ordeal for many. Addressing this issue inherently lies in organizations creating flexible work policies and shifting from traditional working norms to accommodate all their employees' needs.

9.5. From Discouragement to Encouragement: Transforming Education

Finally, the daunting barriers start as early as the classroom for women in tech. Discouragement from peers and mentors alike, unrealistic societal norms, and lack of female role models often lead to decreased enthusiasm. Reigniting the passion in young women to join smart home tech requires a transformation in the educational system, having more female teachers in STEM subjects, and creating nurturing environments that foster innovation without bias.

In sum, the path to progress is a rough one, beset with challenges at every turn. However, these barriers are not insurmountable. The strength, tenacity, and determination demonstrated by women in the smart home technology industry are already leading towards changes. They are indeed breaking the barriers, rebuffing the challenges, paving the way for a gender-balanced, inclusive, and innovation-driven future, forever changing the face of technology one smart home at a time.

Chapter 10. Finding Balance: Personal Stories from Women in the Tech Industry

The chapter begins by exploring the personal narratives of the tireless women, highlighting the arduous journey to attain a semblance of balance in life. Straddling between their integral roles in the technology industry and well beyond, it's a testament of their fortitude and resilience.

10.1. Triumphs and Trials: The Never-ending Learning Curve

Unfolding the intricacies of personal stories, we begin by navigating the labyrinth of professional triumphs and trials. The majority of women spoke of the steep learning curve they had to embrace upon entering the field. This was not just limited to mastering the intricate web of algorithms, coding languages and system designs, but also involved comprehending the subtle workplace dynamics innately skewed towards their male counterparts. The triumphant women iterated that this curve indeed taught them invaluable lessons, lessons that have shaped their careers and fueled their spirit to soldier on.

However, the road to achieving professional prowess was strewn with plentiful trials. The unspoken rule of overcompensation and the constant underestimation of their capabilities stirred troughs of self-doubt and stress. But just as tides oscillate, they found strength in their passion for technology and a resolve to turn the tide of inequality.

10.2. Personal Lives in Perpetual Motion: Striking the Work-Life Balance

While juggling high-pressure jobs, these women never let their professional lives eclipse their personal ones. Jousting the everpresent challenge of maintaining a balance, many candid stories emerged of working motherhood, of times when 24 hours seemed less, times when the pressure to give more at work nibbled at the quality moments spent at home. Yet, through all this, stretched thin and pulled in all directions, they managed to succeed, even if not seamlessly.

Recounting the anecdotes of daily life, it is evident that the quest for work-life balance transforms from being an individual persuit to a collective effort. Supportive partners, understanding managers, and a pliable work culture played a major contributory role in maintaining this intricate balance.

10.3. Wellness, a Silent Casualty: Revisiting Health and Happiness

A resounding theme in all personal narratives was regarding the neglect of health and wellness in their pursuit of success. Stress, often considered an occupational hazard in the tech industry, started to seep into their personal lives, eroding the fundamentals of happiness. Chronic ailments, insomnia, and burnout became the silent casualties of their success.

However, their stories did not end on a grim note. Amidst the dark clouds, rays of resilience shone brightly. Many women took proactive steps to reclaim their wellbeing, highlighting how the industry's responsibility is not merely towards gender inclusivity but also promotes an environment of holistic well-being.

10.4. The Power of Networks: Building Support Systems

A crucial part of maintaining life balance was the role of social networks, both personally and professionally. Joining or organizing women-led tech communities, mentorship programmes, or simply peer-to-peer support provided a gentle cushion against high-stress environments. These networks became sanctuaries of reassurance, a place to share common struggles, exchange advice, and most importantly, to reaffirm their identity and worth as competent professionals within the tech industry.

10.5. The Never-Ending Balancing Act: Navigating the Way Forward

While the journey is challenging and sometimes draining, these women persist, spurred by their love for technology and the desire to reshape the world. The essence of their stories portrays a resolute belief in the possibility of a world where women can thrive in the tech industry without compromising their personal wellbeing.

Through this detailed exploration of their personal stories, our understanding of the experiences and challenges faced by women in the male-dominated tech world deepens. Each of these narratives is composed more of resilience than of struggle, more of hope than despair, vividly painting an empowering picture of their day-to-day experiences. Breaking through the barriers, persisting against odds, and finding their unique balance, these women are not just building smart homes, but also paving the way for a future of greater gender inclusivity within the tech industry.

Chapter 11. The Future is Bright: How Women are Reshaping the Technology Roadmap

As we embark on our elaborative conclusion, let's first take a moment to acknowledge the profound journey that has led us here - an odyssey from humble beginnings to a narrative of impressive innovation, brimming with courage, discovery, resilience, and unyielding ambition. It is here that we delve into the bright and promising tale of how women are actively redefining the smart home technology playbook.

11.1. Protagonists of Progress: Women Pioneers in Technology

As we fast-forward to the dawn of the 21st century, an exciting new era with a fresh focus on technological innovations is taking shape. As driving forces behind this exciting transformation, women have made significant strides, superbly navigating the amplitude of formidable challenges, complex technology jargon, and a maze of circuit-boards. They are crafting a revolution in domains traditionally dominated by men, unveiling new technologies to equip households with the convenience and security to match the fast-paced modern lifestyle. The emergence of these trailblazing women marks an epochal shift in the tech industry. Their dedicated efforts are piecing together a future, where technology and living spaces seamlessly merge, offering enriched lives fueled by smart utilities.

Women in technology are not a rarity; in fact, their qualified presence has now become an imperative factor in shaping the progression of our digital future. They have blazed a remarkable trail as developers, coders, testers, designers, entrepreneurs, and tech CEOs. These fearless females are taking the helm and swimming in deep waters to lay the bricks for the triumphant castle of smart home technology.

11.2. Intelligent Abodes: Women Leading Home Innovation

An evolving generation of women innovators and entrepreneurs are cresting the wave of home automation. Operating from an embodied sense of initiative and innovation, they are overturning stumbling blocks into stepping-stones in the pipeline to progress. The spectrum of their technological prowess ranges from perceptive digital assistants, new-fangled appliances synchronization, energy and climate management, to advanced security systems. Their technological wizardry caters to a vast gamut of applications, redefining our domiciliary experiences.

The arenas of home automation and smart home technology have found their champions in these women. Their ground-breaking innovations are hailed and respected for offering comprehensive home management solutions at the tip of the fingers or at the sound of a voice command. They have carved a niche where technology is a thoughtful integrator, promoter of comfort, convenience, and safety, rather than an intrusive, unwanted foreign body.

In times of strife such as the global pandemic, the importance of these smart solutions for homes came to fore. The transition to work from home culture was made seamless and manageable by numerous smart tools designed by women such as Zoom, Slack and more. There hasn't been a more pronounced validation of the impact and significance of women contributions in this realm.

11.3. Advancing Past the Obstacles: Women Rising Against the Odds

Despite facing innumerable obstacles, these individuals, armed with unwavering determination and vision, have transcended societal norms and gender stereotypes. They have selected paths, known more for their thorns than their roses, and for each bruise they've suffered, they have bloomed into roses themselves. Be it challenging the sexist norms or fighting the systemic bias within the tech industry, they have come out victorious and have emerged pivoting towards a more equal future. Their footprints on these thorny paths are filled with inspiration serving as guidance for the future generation of girls planning to venture into technology and its many branches.

11.4. Shaping Tomorrow: The Path Ahead

Looking ahead, it is comforting to fathom a journey, handcrafted by these revolutionary women, that deconstructs boundaries and breathes life into the realm of dormant possibilities. They are not only instigating a quiet upheaval in the world of smart home technology but are also embodying the changing construct of technology innovation that welcomes and embraces their perspectives.

Their consistent and relentless strides are vibrant testimony to their tireless efforts of laying solid groundwork for a future where household tech solutions will become an essential life element. Their vision for the future is a world where our homes become our allies. A world where assistive technology serves up the potential to create more time for meaningful engagement and contributes to enhanced living experiences.

In conclusion, the narrative of women in smart home technology is a stirring testament to audacity and innovation. They have catalyzed a movement, which is continuously evolving, while also inspiring millions around the globe. As we delve into an increasingly tech-driven future, there's no doubt that these pioneering women will continue to pilot and set new standards, further invigorating the smart home technology landscape. Their progressive visions and dynamic leadership paint a promising scenario, signifying that indeed, the future is bright!

www.ingramcontent.com/pod-product-compliance
Lightning Source LLC
Chambersburg PA
CBHW070955220526
45471CB00007B/3040